The Book of Noah

The Book of Noah

poems

Yoni Hammer-Kossoy

GRAYSON BOOKS
West Hartford, Connecticut
graysonbooks.com

The Book of Noah
Copyright © 2023 by Yoni Hammer-Kossoy
Published by Grayson Books
West Hartford, Connecticut
ISBN: 979-8-9855442-6-8
Library of Congress Control Number: 2023933380

Interior & Cover Design: Cindy Stewart
Author Photo: Rebecca Kowalsky

Contents

Evening Prayer

This is how it feels
to be a forest: each tree alone
within reach of another

each tree bent from holding up
the sky. Sometimes a great wind
blows and all the trees sway

sometimes there's a hush
and only one seems to move
from an unseen breath.

Ark

Dear Noah

The days stack like coins on a scale and summer tips toward another end. You feel it in the August heat. You hear it in the burr of cicadas and flap of sparrows snatching grapes from a stunted vine in the garden. I used to think people talk about weather because they're afraid of silence, but what did you say when you came in for dinner, sawdust on your shoulders and stuck in your beard, and your wife said, please that's enough. Don't tell me your generation refused to see the towering anvil clouds even after it started raining, and I won't tell you it's too late for mine. I am trying to find a voice that doesn't push away, that hews close to beauty, but my optimism has become like a last rhino in captivity. We have forests and towns that combust under a fist of sun, we have mosaics of dread laid one tessera by one. We have satellites winking far above, supercomputers predicting short-term doom and long-term destruction. I am calling out to you, Noah, because you saw everything wash away and begin again, because I want to know if there's more to do now than build a bigger boat and keep a neater zoo.

Waiting for the Rain

This time Noah dreamed the flood came
too soon. He was hunched over a quartered tree
adze in hand, chipping away another beam
when the first drops sizzled down
and he knew it would never stop.
A goat wandered by wearing the head
of a bear, and cackled like his neighbors.
He heard the rasp of his grandson
as the waters thickened
leaving no place of purchase.
He wanted the dream to end
the way he wanted all waiting to end,
arid sky in the back of his throat
deepening doubt of a lifetime
the planks of his body sealed with dust.

Ark

Praise the plastic backyard shed
for the way it welcomes cracked stars
and fallen apricot blossoms two-by-two
into the shelter of its dusty walls,
for the rusted grill in one corner
and the bruised tricycle in another,
for the beach chairs that were once royal green,
for the basketball and volleyball and football and the pump
that could restore their swagger if I only had the right needle,
for the hedge clippers leftover from before the basement flooded,
for what is somehow the neighbor's dog leash—
even though his dog died twelve years ago,
for the garden hose wound on its unruly spool,
for the crate of clothing marked give away,
for the bucket of paint that doesn't match any bedroom walls
and for the shed's cover that never stays shut
unless a few bags of topsoil are piled high
holding everything snug as months and years drift by.

Sledgehammer Blues

They've been drilling since half past seven like a national sport
and I groan, knowing I can kiss this summer's quiet goodbye.
Somehow my neighbor forgot to mention the renovations when
I saw him load a suitcase into his car and drive away. When
we redid our place, we sent offerings of cookies and wine and
abundant apologies in advance. I remember the workers yelled
to each other even when they were taking a break, as if their
bodies couldn't shake the uproar of building. I remember one guy
who fussed over his coffee but looked beatific when he hefted a
sledgehammer. Drywall, plaster, cinderblocks, window casings,
nothing stood a chance against his ministrations. If only my
life could be as straight-up as knocking things down and letting
someone else sweep away the rubble. I yearned to take a swing but
never mustered the nerve to ask because I knew he'd just laugh.
And you Noah, what about your neighbors? Did they demand to
know what's going on and how long it would take? At what point
did you stop trying to explain what a flooded world meant? Year
after year they must have railed against the clamor as the ark grew
under your hands. Year after year, who can blame them for jeering
and cursing you as the sky stayed stubborn and cloudless blue.

I am mute as a gopher tree

The wind blows and I shake my branches at a blank sky. If only fire would sweep this hillside so I could sing. I am the man who planted me, little boy at his side; the grandson who comes back, axe in hand. I am the axe, the keen edge, the unmaker, the reshaper. I am the fall, forever falling, felled. I am the green relief from standing. I am the wedge, the mallet, the split that solves the puzzle of opening me. Here are my rings, densely spaced, uncountable; here is my heartwood, first to be discarded, soft and twisted after years of tracking the sun. I am the second cut that leaves me in quarters, the slow work that shapes me into beams, into planks. I am the calloused hands, the stick of sap, the long paths of grain joined in place, the dimming memory of rain in whorls and sanded knots. The ark is sealed tight but has no rudder. I am not what I dreamed I might be.

Dreambirds

1.
They fly alone or in flocks.
Sometimes there's a wing clap
or feathers left behind.
One sun-capped morning
three blue eggs begin to hatch
under my pillow
but when I wake
it's the middle of the night.

2.
I wish I could explain
these hauntings, wish there was
a pressing deadline
some oddity to account
for their appearance.
I do the dishes, take out
the trash, go to sleep.

3.
Cuckoos are timely liars.
Canaries sing soothing ballads.
A vulture heralds spiritual growth,
so does a swan. Stray sparrows
bring news to your window.
An eagle will carry you
to great heights. See bright parrots
and get ready to travel.
Leave a trail of breadcrumbs
to overcome disappointment.

4.
I undress an onion
and it makes me cry.
When I look down
all my fingers are intact
but the onion has become
a crow, pinned to the cutting board.

5.
Unease burns off
by breakfast.
Gourmet coffee and rolls
in the kitchenette.
Neon post-its on walls.
I say good morning
and my office mate says
nothing could be better.

6.
Ranks of planted pines.
Sunlight buzzes
through broken canopy.
In the understory
tight fists of seed
wait in vain for flame.

7.
I go to the post office at lunch
and feel lost by the break
in routine. The air is a hard slap
against browning trees.
Someone leans on his horn

not knowing about the accident
up the street. At the crosswalk
it says my request to cross is received
but the light doesn't change.

8.
Taking a shower
the soap keeps slipping.
When it flies to the ceiling
a new bar is back in my hands.
Later I brush my teeth
and the bathroom is steamed
with doves. I've never seen birds
fly this way.

9.
A year on, they're still digging
at the building site.
How much silence
have they rent from bedrock?
When does a bulldozer driver
stop trembling after a shift?
I see pixels flying
from my laptop
and wish I made glass mugs for a living.
I can drink jasmine tea from mugs
warm my hands on them
throw them at walls
and listen to them shatter.

10.
A man on a brick building
with a flock of pigeons.

You stop and point,
explain they are fighting pigeons.
He conducts them
like a ragged orchestra:
when he raises his arms
the birds burst up from the roof
and when he lowers them
the sky clatters home to roost.

Dear Noah

The flood rose for weeks, unlike anything you could imagine. Flood of numbers, flood of silence. The way sleet changes to snow with a sudden lack of pelting. Flood of astonished lines on a test. Flood of thoughts misplaced like keys. We became cutout dolls at the window, listening to shouts of kids playing under a pink sky. Home was an ark with a flood in its throat.

Topside

When it's not too stormy Noah likes to go topside and shuffle along the slick planks, inspecting his kingdom of pewter sky and roiling sea. Anything's better than staying below with its stench and endless list of things to care about. In the beginning there were bloated bodies, felled trees, shattered roofs, all the jetsam of what once was, although now he's more likely to see nothing, or at most, a distant slap of a whale's fluke. Some days he wonders if he ever wants the rain to end, until he remembers the possibilities of a buzzing spring morning: sun painting his upturned face, woosh of wing on a wavering branch, a redbreast's four-note defiance.

Still Life with Unrolled Awning

The awning, like my heart, is cheerful with its green and white stripes. A bowl of dusty grapes has been cleared leaving a laptop and two teacups distanced on the tablecloth. We are too late for whatever happened, too early for what happens next. A cicada rubs its eyes and peonies wait in their pots. Even accomplished painters find this afternoon light difficult to capture. The awning fidgets in the breeze, tugging at bolts. I hope someone remembers to roll it in before bedtime. Some nights the wind settles, but when it barrels through from far away, the whole building lifts from its foundation, sailing off in a shower of broken pipes and stone.

Mrs. Noah Counts the Flying Creatures

She hates it when he slaps at mosquitos in bed.
She tells him it's better to save his outrage for God
or that he'll go deaf beating up his ears, but only
when she says it's ruining her sleep does he decide
it might be wiser to stop and suffer quietly
as they pilot paths of their breath in the dark.

He thought it was such a great idea to build
a vaulted chamber for the flying creatures
but whaddya know, only the mosquitos stayed
while the rest swooped in and out of the ark.

Now his latest vision of a fast and grotesque future,
burning forests and talking screens.
So many people, he cries, but she takes solace
in the birds and bats and flies
and—yes—mosquitos too, that survived,
all swarming in minor galaxies.

Inside the Ark

A full parking lot and a pogo stick. A gourmet meal and a paper mask. A minuet in G for kazoo and trombone. Marriage and picking a melon. A bonfire and a manicured lawn. Searchlights at a movie opening and a dimmer switch. A five-year-old driving an SUV. This actually happened. The cops pulled him over miles from home and he said he was on his way to buy a Ferrari. Thinking fast and thinking slow. I rub my sneakers on the rug and spark you on the nose. Daydreams and deadlines. My head and a pineapple. A wine's vintage and the glass I pour at dinner. Was it hotter that summer? Terroir and a lotto ticket. A colony of bats and a roller derby. Staying in the ark and leaving the cave. All that flame built up and the house it wants to burn down.

Thirst

It's always there waiting
when the day's tasks are done,
but tonight Noah tapped the last cask of wine

and now he tosses in bed
heart thudding, adrift in his body,
wondering how it will last.

He'll need to stay busy longer
until the murmur of lapping waves
might slip him into sleep

or let him yearn for the rub
of dirt between his fingers
while planting the vines he stowed away.

Stars bloom far above the clouds,
manta rays haunt the phosphorescent depths.
The ark groans around him.

Dear Noah

When the rain finally stopped did you wake with a start or oversleep? Did you laze under a lacy shawl of dreams, pressed against your wife, forgetting about to-do lists and the vast surrounding emptiness? Did you count pinpoints of light pushing through wallboards and connect them into constellations? Even the animals must have been unmoored by the silence spreading like a sudden contagion, by the awareness of multitudes jostling in the stoppered dark. Gone was the hammering of sky and flailing waves, replaced by a texture of air you had almost forgotten. This is what a murmuration of starlings sounds like when it turns without one wing scraping the next. This is what keeps hand-hewn stones in the shape of stairs. In that moment between before and after did you whisper *what next?* or did you know, the way one breath follows another, this was all part of a plan? Now when I wake to the spatter of drops on my window it feels like consolation. I count rivers between lightning and thunder as I've done since I was young. The only flood I fear is time.

The Smell of Rain

But there was never a simple way to call the smell of rain until 1964, when two Australian scientists coined *petrichor*, combining Greek for stone and blood of the gods.

Petrichor was eventually tied to an organic compound called geosmin, which gets thrown into the air when water droplets hit dry ground and plants. People can detect geosmin in traces as low as 400 parts per trillion, meaning human beings are more attuned to the smell of rain than a shark is to blood.

They say the human nose can smell a trillion combinations of odors. They say a bloodhound's nose is ten- to-one-hundred-million times more sensitive than a human's, capable of following a missing child's trail into the past, if not the future.

I try to grasp one trillion, but like yearning, it's either too big or too small to comprehend. There are one trillion galaxies in a stripe of midnight sky. There are one trillion molecules of water in the tiniest drop of rain.

I ask the internet about the purpose of smell and it tells me to go for a walk in the rain. It tells me anosmia means loss of smell, which sounds like insomnia or amnesia, and makes me think of forgetting how to sleep, forgetting everything I know.

The first thing Noah does when he leaves the ark is build an altar and offer sacrifices. But he never weeps. In the Bible it says God smells the pleasing odor and promises not to destroy the world again, and I think of philosophers wrangling for centuries over such brazen anthropomorphism with no comment about Noah's dry-eyed silence. I think of how namelessly good the air must have smelled the day when light drizzle became the flood.

On the last night of summer, I lie awake as the wind flips the neighbor's laundry rack and rattles the backyard trees. Months of pent-up dust and heat disperse in a snap. Rain spatters through the open window and I breathe in the smell like a promise.

Seed

Everything holds a seed of its undoing

the way a light bulb waits to explode
in the dark. In the warp of a chair
there's a bonfire. In a bowl of lentils,
shooting stars. In a heap of stones
the razed keep's last stand. In a splay of bones
what was once a man, the body's wick, its short fuse.
In curves of cliffs swirls a crumbling story.
Dirges clatter in a pinwheel, a window crack shrieks
with the hurtling world. In a cloudburst falls the rain
it can't bear. In a sepia photo all the years it must.
In every offhand word lurk leftover goodbyes.
My voice is thrown, I hardly move my lips.
They uncrumple like a tossed plastic bag.
In every movie there's a credit roll
like last gasps of sunset at the beach.
If it doesn't end as expected, there's comfort
in the crawl of cast and production teams,
special thanks, anything to sit a little longer
in a final swell of soundtrack, not worrying
if there's a sequel. In a parked car ticks an empty engine.
On a limp line hangs a lost week's washing
and the night sighs sick with blooming silence.
Jasmine. Batwings. A moon full of used dreams.

Dear Noah

The days and weeks stack like coins on a scale and perhaps this year will be different. You can feel it in the turn from winter to spring coming like an undeserved but unrefuted reprieve. Early mornings sound like an aviary stuffed full of bright plumed birds and if I reach high enough, I might touch the world's dome painted with stars. The snails that came out skating after yesterday's rain must have known it was their last chance for months. Suddenly trees have bodies again, giving shape and sound to a rising tide of wind. The grape vine grows six inches overnight, grabbing the laundry line in brawny tendrils, unfurling leaves like sails. I'm ready for them to take me away, somewhere, anywhere, out of myself, out of the ark I've painstakingly built, into a future where everything is still possible.

Memory Foam

—after Heraclitus

River me   rush over me   midnight memory   star scabbled
time me   pressing down   hold me   underwater me   same
bed never me   same water never me   moment to moment
every weight bearing moment me   every foam cell murmuring
every riverbed another me   Noah in his ark me   unasleep me
unasleep olive tree   tearing holes in sky me   God remembers
Noah   God remembers Rachel   God remembers unasleep in
Egypt me   so much remembering   memoryscapes sneaking
up on me   never forget   fancy bed forgetting me   unasleep
me   fancy eyes forget to see me   too much river forgetting
opens her womb   ice age presses down   holding me down
opens his ark   too much unasleep night in me   unasleep river
rushes me   last stand icemelt   command to leave his ark me
last mountains rise up   forgetting bed me   unasleep river
rushing in me   same never   river   me

Exit

When I left the job, I didn't look back,
writing and erasing programs for sixteen years
I took everything from my desk in an old knapsack

a floppy hat, empty notebooks, a box of thumbtacks
two company mugs good for coffee and beer.
When I left the job, I didn't look back.

On the lobby TV: breaking news of Arctic icepack
melting fast, raising scientists' fears—
I carried my bruises in an old knapsack.

(Quick cut to palm-treed paradise lacking
a seawall and likely to disappear.)
Would anything be different if I went back?

Outside the sun lingered on its saffron track
and a crow shuffled off a habit of stairs.
I took everything from my desk in an old knapsack.

What more to say? No codes were cracked,
humanity wasn't saved, fortune's smile never appeared.
When I left the job, I didn't look back.
I carried everything I had in an old knapsack.

Sea Squill in the Garden

All year the sea squill lay in the ground
between rose bushes and a stone wall
exactly where the kids planted it
with great fanfare, an onion-sized bulb
cradled in both hands, famous for its bulk
and end of summer bloom. All year
it lay there like a whale's heart
beating two or three times a minute
while the world above spun
from current events to home remodeling,
despots and interior designers united in desire
to tear down and rebuild in their own image.
All year it lay in the dark, silent enough
to be forgotten, and no one can say
whether it developed a taste for tea with lemon
or 19th century novels or if the roses
minded having such a quiet neighbor.
And no one said a word when its stem didn't grow
and its flowers didn't unfurl
to the plum wind of shortening days.
All year it lay there, not dead but dormant,
gathering for a leap into light.

Outside the Ark

I am a lump of river clay centered on a spinning wheel.
That is, the rain has stopped. That is,
I am walking to the store, weight flowing heel to toe,
trying to stay outside of thought.
Bird chatter and a wash of jasmine.
Two cars parked front to front with jumper cables.
A siren warbles in the distance.

So much depends on that first throw,
it almost always lands off-center.
Almost everything I've learned
is how to caress the less than ideal into place
how enough pressure between fingertips
slicks away layer after layer.

Prayer for Applying Sunscreen

Lord of cobalt sky
and crumbling ozone,
grant me the patience to smear
this clotted offering of cream
with care and dignity
and trust its polymers
to work their chemical wonders
as I venture outside.
Let me not miss a spot,
especially where I once did,
let it spread silky-clean
along the creased map of my body,
from the single-digit highways
of arms and legs
to the sleepy cul-de-sacs of earlobes
and toes. Let it stay out of my eyes
as sweat seeps from beneath
the hat brim's wide scowl.
And after many unflinching hours
let me remember to reapply
so that I may remain
safe in my skin
from any harvest the sun will sow.

To a Thirty-Foot Statue of Lenin Surrounded by Weeds in the Sculpture Garden of a Bulgarian Museum

Things could be worse, that stripe of bird shit on your back could have landed smack between chiseled cheekbone and stern eye. They could have bulldozed you, pulverized you, sold you pound by pebbled pound for landscaping. Gods have always been defaced and erased by victors, and considering the amount of blood splashed at your feet, this deal feels like early retirement with a sea view. Maybe all monuments should be treated this way —quietly, there to be ignored or visited and left behind. Removed from grand plazas and parades, sent out back with the other weathered slabs of bronze and granite, you are finally smaller than life. I suppose it could be shadier or the signage to find you clearer, but the halo of bees humming about certainly appreciate the flowering weeds. Does their collective wealth of clover honey make you crack a smile when nobody is looking? I wish I had a good way of explaining selfies to you. I wish I could tell you the revolution made things better, or the counter-revolution, or the revolution after that. I won't ask if it gets lonely this side of history. I hope the folds of your cloak hold the sun's heat long after nightfall.

Self-Portrait with Fainting Star

Rumors of Betelgeuse's impending death have been greatly exaggerated. The red supergiant star appears to be in no danger of imminently exploding, even though a recent, dramatic dip in brightness hinted that it could be on its last legs. The latest observations reveal instead that the star is starting to regain its former light.
—National Geographic Magazine, February 26, 2020

I like that your name is pronounced *beetle juice* like the movie
from my youth; that I know how to find you,
high in the winter night where Orion hunts the giant bull;
that even now I can taste the cold that crackled in my throat
when I dragged a birthday telescope outside
and aimed it beyond the city glare. I like that astronomers
called this recent downturn *a fainting* as if stars swoon and have
bad days. I like that they couldn't explain why,
and now that it stopped, now that you have begun
to right yourself from whatever dust or cosmic cycle
worried your brow, I like that many are disappointed
nothing else is likely to happen soon. I like that you,
like most other giants, come complete with dramatic end;
that it's a cataclysm safely viewed from 650 light years away.
And when you finally blow, next month or in a thousand years,
I like that you will light up the sky brighter than the moon
and stay that way for weeks, blurting out a secret
of what already happened centuries ago.

To Last Night's Mosquito

According to the latest calculations there are 36 planets crackling with intelligent life in the Milky Way, and if one of them happens to make contact today I'll probably shrug with exhaustion after last night's carnage. I slapped and swayed, I pounded and prayed, and I'm still lying here at 4:57 am, welted and wilted, listening to every bird in southern Jerusalem wake up at once. You brute, you bulldozer, why must you shoulder through the window screen? It gives me no solace to admire your longstanding sliver of natural history—that's my blood on your Jurassic lips—and I'd gladly show you the door, or wall, or any other solid object if I could spot you whizzing around. But you've flown off to lay eggs in the afterglow of your feast. And I'm left with a muggy commute, lusting for a nap, so I can dream of sleeping somewhere too cold for mosquitos to live.

Dust Libation

The clay pot always pops into mind when I'm prompted to describe an object. It's not for lack of other stuff with sentimental heft to choose from—the cool cheek of a lucky rock, the bleached hues of a polaroid snapped one vacation cruise, homebound errata jumping up and down like school kids blurting pick me, pick me—but one look at the pot collecting dust on a high shelf, its unglazed curves, its charred edges, its chipped lip, and you know it's not old but wandering-in-the-desert ancient. And when I tell the tale of Moshe Dayan gifting it to my grandfather, I love the ooohs and aaahs that slip out of peoples' mouths—see the old grifter's signature on its base, that's right, 600 BCE, think of all the years erased between then and now. And the thing is, I've written too many half-fired poems about this pot but never know how to finish them, those moon-shaped notches someone left on the handle's arc, those skips and ticks of archeology dulling into unsolvable ache, so just this once what I'm going to do is throw it on the ground and walk away.

If Superheroes Wrote Sonnets

When I was your age, I loved the shocked glare
on a bad guy's kisser if I landed
in media res, red cape aflutter,
and stopped his speeding bullets bare-handed.
It was everything a hero could crave:
justice, adventure, a steady paycheck,
pain-free knees. No need to prove I was brave,
didn't sweat the future or lack for respect.
Lately super-hearing lets me eavesdrop
on what might come next—long walks in the park
mynas wheeling and dealing from treetops,
pale days piling into another week.
I know you have everything figured out
because once I had it all figured out.

A Hand in the Dark

Carefully, a secret
      being whispered to no one
           from birth.
Unless I stumble or fall, and some-
      times
           I want to tell. I get by
under streetlights but

need a hand in the dark.
      Photoreceptors flutter,
           dry leaves
in an unsteady breeze. Do you know
      fire
           flickers from pupil to lens
to the retina

in the blink of an eye
      my brain breaks down the jigsaw
           puzzle
of your face. Do you know bright sunshine
      skids
           between steel motes of static?
It's not what you think.

There is absence where you
      stand, an untuned radar beam
           flash pops
and murk a crouching on the edges
      like
           dry itch from a phantom limb.

Don't we all get by?

What scares me is the slow
       decline. Less, is less, is less.
            Pity
is a werewolf under starless sky.
       Sight
              a chain of islands erased
by indifferent tide

and midday fog. Oh jot
       and slang and missing letter
            slippage
from who to why, one genetic bit
       scores
              the translucent lie between
seeing and going blind.

A Bow in the Clouds

In His Generation

Noah was a righteous man, he was blameless in his generation.
—*Genesis 6:9*

1.

I was running late, and I was running for the bus, which was lumbering along in midday traffic. I had a chance to catch it if I could get across the road, but of course, just as I got to the crosswalk the light turned a hard red. In the span of a second, I felt my brain run the cost-benefit analysis on possible death by oncoming garbage truck and decide that waiting in the sun for another twenty minutes would be more annoying. I made a break for it, remembering all those quarters I lost playing *Frogger* as a kid, and gave a little cheer when, all limbs intact on the other side, I saw that I would get to the bus stop first. Which is exactly when two police officers stepped out and busted me for jaywalking.

They were there admiring my foolish performance the whole time and given how intent I was on catching the bus, I'm lucky I didn't plow right into them. As it was, I did stop, and groaned helplessly when they asked for ID and the bus crawled away into the distance. Officer one ducked into the patrol car to verify that I wasn't an escaped murderer while her partner, old enough to be counting down the days to retirement, lit a cigarillo and scolded me over the grave danger I had just put myself and others into. I should have kept my mouth shut, but said, *You know that's really bad for my health.* Which he acknowledged with a nod, and stepping a few paces away, said *That's why I'm smoking over here.*

2.

Who would you rather be, Noah, or Abraham? The question almost reminds me of the Superman vs. Spiderman arguments my kids had with their friends, except those battles could go on for hours without a clear winner ever being declared. When I ask people which biblical figure they identify with, the answer is always Abraham—and apart from his occasional confusion between *sister* and *wife*, and one rather traumatic camping trip with his son Isaac, I suppose I get it. Abraham is the paragon of faith and kindness, and when called upon, arguing with God. He's the father of not one, but two religions; a savvy businessman and brave fighter; an immigrant who left his family and risked everything; in short, a mover and shaker who answered the divine call and changed history forever.

But what about Noah? I understand why Abraham is so great, but I'm still not sure what turns people off to Noah. Didn't he follow God's command to the letter? Didn't he build the ark, and save humanity and all living creatures from destruction? Doesn't the Bible say he was righteous and blameless? At this point everyone, somehow, seems to know the midrash's answer: Noah was righteous and blameless *in his generation*; had he lived in a time with someone like Abraham or Moses he wouldn't have amounted to anything much at all.

3.

One morning, not long after paying my ticket and debt to society, I'm thinking about Noah while I make my rounds of the neighborhood recycling bins. It's already unbearably hot—with record temperatures forecast for at least another week—and by the time I've put a few weeks of accumulated paper, plastic, and glass in their proper receptacles I'm good and sweaty. It doesn't bother me that much; I need the exercise, and more importantly, through this act of putting plastic bottles in a brightly painted metal cage, I can imagine that I am personally stopping apocalyptic warming from melting Greenland, flooding coastal cities from New York to Shanghai, and driving all wildlife to extinction (except for the hardiest cockroaches and crows).

Or perhaps not. The rational side of my brain knows I can't reverse all of the industrial revolution's environmental havoc by properly disposing empty beer bottles. It even recognizes that the problems of climate change and pollution are only partially related. But I'm struck by how convinced I am that my personal actions are making the world a better place. Globally, humans produce more than 2 billion tons of waste a year, including nearly 300 million tons of plastic. And so recycling, along with its sister Rs of reduce and reuse, has evolved over the years into an effective way of *doing something.*

Except here's where things start to get complicated. Recently I read that the Jerusalem Municipality invested 100 million shekels in a waste processing plant to separate recyclable materials from all of the city's garbage. Since 2019, this plant has been sorting 2,000 tons of trash a day, sending paper, metal, plastic, and organic material to various customers and middlemen around the country. One could argue this is a much more efficient way to deal with the city's recycling challenge, and indeed, there's now talk of removing some, if not all of the collection bins from neighborhood streets. But where does that leave me or anyone else wanting to do the right thing? I've always harbored suspicions that my carefully separated bottles were simply being carted off to a dump behind my back. Now I'm supposed to throw everything in the trash and hope for the best?

4.

According to the midrash, 120 years passed from when God commanded Noah to build the ark until the flood actually took place. During this time, Noah planted a forest, watched it grow, harvested the wood, and constructed the ark. This was so that his neighbors might stop by and ask *hey Noah, what's up?* and upon hearing the news of *impending* world destruction, change their wicked ways.

I suppose impending is the tricky word in the context of the midrash's 120 years, just as nowadays, predictions of climate doom by 2100 are so difficult to picture and even more difficult to act on. Eco-philosopher Timothy Morton calls global warming a *hyperobject*, something that is so large, so widely distributed, and at the same time interconnected, that it defies normal paths of definition and perception. Trying to understand the difference between 1.5 or 2 or more degrees Celsius of warming, all of the meshed causes and effects that lead to and come from it, are just the tip of the melting hyperobject iceberg. Nevertheless, as Morton puts it, "I can't see it. I can't touch it. But I know it exists, and I know I'm a part of it. I should care about it."

I do care about global warming, but I wish I had a better idea of what I should be doing about it. Just as I wish it was clearer what Noah was doing during all that time before the flood. He wasn't secretly hoarding food and supplies like a prepper before the next pandemic. On the other hand, how effective was he in trying to change peoples' minds? I think of Greta Thunberg imploring world leaders to change the status quo on carbon emissions, and in the absence of any progress, declaring: "All political and economic systems have failed, but humanity has not yet failed." And then I think of how in the midrash, people were still mocking Noah even as the animals paraded into the ark, even as the first drops of rain started to fall.

5.

I'm old enough to remember when soda and beer cans had ring tabs that pulled off when opened. I used to collect them at the beach in a pickle jar, along with green and brown sea glass and shells, and loved the jangly music they made when shaken together. I remember Smoky the Bear telling people, *Only you can prevent forest fires*, although that slogan had been around for a few decades by the time I was born. And I remember watching cartoons and being transfixed by commercials showing Iron Eyes Cody crying on the banks of a trash-filled river. I knew nothing about the politics behind the ad—the Keep America Beautiful organization that produced it was founded in 1953 by the American Can Co. and the Owens-Illinois Glass Co., and later joined by the likes of Coca-Cola and the Dixie Cup Co.—but it turns out this was a sly push to deflect attention away from beverage corporations being required to use recyclable containers. And I couldn't imagine how well my generation and generations to come would internalize the hobbling message of personal responsibility taking precedence over collective political action and corporate accountability. All I remember is the deep-voiced narrator saying: *People start pollution. People can stop it.*

Fast forward a few decades, and is it really such a big surprise to discover that it was an ad exec who supposedly coined the term *carbon footprint*, or that BP supposedly rolled out the first carbon offset calculator in 2004? As long as the focus remains on guilty consumers finding ways to live a climate-conscious lifestyle, pumps and profits can keep on flowing indefinitely.

6.

The Talmud teaches that the world is filled with *mazikin*, or demons. It quotes Abba Binyamin, who says, "If the eye was given permission to see, no creature would be able to withstand the abundance and ubiquity of the demons and continue to live unaffected by them." According to Abaye, "They are more numerous than we are and they stand over us like mounds of earth surrounding a pit." Rav Huna goes even further: "Each and every one of us has a thousand demons to his left and ten thousand to his right." It even says you can put the ashes of the "afterbirth of a firstborn female black cat, born to a firstborn female black cat" on your eyes in order to see these demons—but beware, "Rav Beivai bar Abaye performed this procedure, saw the demons, and was harmed." Only after the sages prayed for mercy on his behalf was he able to recover.

I've often read this passage to be a reflection of the rabbis grappling with the fragility of life. If we could truly see the dangers of the world, then we'd never be able to move out of constant fear. Therefore people live in a default state of blindness, which is what makes it possible to do things like get married, have kids, invent things, or even make a run for the bus.

But substitute *environmental awareness* for danger, and I wonder if now these demons become a way to ask about the habits and lifestyles of modern times. As in: if we could actually see the environmental impact of our daily actions, could we ever really live?

7.

There is a second, less quoted opinion in the midrash about Noah. One that gives me reason to pause: *Look how righteous Noah was in his generation, had he lived with Abraham or Moses he would have achieved even greater heights!* The power of individuals to lift up others through their actions, and for the collective to be strengthened by it, is a message I hope the possible Noahs of our time will hear. That this is said in the name of Resh Lakish, a highway bandit who overcame his past to become one of the great rabbinic scholars in his generation, is certainly not a coincidence.

This is Plastics

found and recycled from the Plastic Industry Association's website thisisplatics.com

People aren't blogging about plastics   keeping kids healthy and safe. They aren't tweeting   about millions of jobs.   They're talking about plastic bag bans   landfills   BPA   phthalates. Cherry-picked data won't solve plastic waste.   For a sustainable future, we need   more plastic – not less.   Plastic packaging is vital   to reducing food insecurity.   Up to 40% less fuel is used   to transport plastic bottles.   A plastic straw   has 60% less global warming potential.   The US plastics industry is responsible   for over one million jobs   over $430 billion annually.   Many plastic products   are designed to be used only once.   No matter the product proper disposal   is key making sure no plastics end up   where they shouldn't.   Plastics make National Parks   even more   environmentally friendly. Every day is Earth Day with the help of plastics.

Motherlode

Pick a laptop, any laptop. Maybe a cherry-red gaming deck
or a drab workhorse, plucked from the dumpster

behind a corporate tower or from the spider-worn corner
of an attic. It doesn't matter. All devices are created equal

on the bed of a recycler's junk truck—they are plastic bricks
to be picked apart; globalized supply lines to be untied;

1200 kilos of earth once dug, crushed, sorted, smelted, purified
and now spent of their engineered magic, ready to be re-mined.

Remove the screws to reveal a motherlode: chipsets, circuit
boards, capacitors, wires, pinpoint soldering, a heat sink,

a hard drive, a touch screen. What nimble fingers can't unlock
the bite of acid and flame force open to extract copper,

silver, platinum, palladium, nickel, titanium, zinc, and more.
Some metals in this scrap yard haul never shake their origin story

of child labor and war, but it is an outrage the market bears
for without cobalt, batteries run down faster; without tungsten,

cellphones won't vibrate; without tin, computer parts split up;
without tantalum and gold, there is no portability or speed.

Some rare-earths like europium, gallium, germanium, rhodium,
ruthenium, and yttrium, are needed for their exotic capacity

of magnetism and durability. When there's no other way to eat
the world's dregs can be harvested a few dollars at a time

in bits and scraps, flakes and traces. The pinnacle of piecework,
it's a fortune in slow motion measured by the ton.

Copper

Before the rains set in; before you read this, trailing a finger through dust on a touch-screen; before a circuit closes and a spark leaps; before a laptop arrives by overnight delivery; before it sails for 24 days from Taipei through the Suez Canal, clears customs, sits in a supply warehouse; before a motherboard slots into form-factored place; before a six-foot wheel of wire is milled to hair-fine strands; before semi-fabricators in southern China cast 99.99% pure copper into sheets and tubes and spools; before it is smelted and refined from 30% concentrates in Jiangxi; before reaching Shanghai after crossing the Pacific Ocean in 31 days on a 347 meter-long cargo ship; before 100,000 tons are dried and dumped into 350 containers stacked five high; before it is pumped 170 kilometers through a nine-inch-diameter pipeline to the Coloso port; before it's crushed and ground and concentrated to slurry; before the 0.7% grade ore is blasted and hauled out of a 600-meter deep pit-mine employing almost three thousand people; before climbing into the thin air of the Atacama Desert in Northern Chile; before any other metal, there is copper, sending out its burnished glint, from the bronze age edge of a sword to the conquering crackle of all things electric.

Carbon

It's 25 degrees Celsius outside this morning when I sit down to write.

Although I grew up in one of the last countries of the world to use Fahrenheit, I know that 25 degrees Celsius is not too hot and not too cold.

For many years I needed to convert Celsius to Fahrenheit in my head, multiplying by 9/5 and adding 32 to figure out if I would need to wear a sweater later in the day.

It's possible you've never even heard of Fahrenheit, that when you're reading this, those last few countries have given it up, or don't exist, but for what it's worth 25 degrees is 77 degrees Fahrenheit, the slightly warm end of *room temperature.*

Here *room temperature* is perhaps not very informative given the limitless variety and locations of those rooms, the comfort preferences of people in them, and the fact that I'm talking about the current weather outside.

Nevertheless, most people would agree that as temperatures go, 25 degrees Celsius makes for a pleasant day: sunny, clear blue sky, a gentle breeze, some bird chatter.

It would still be a pleasant day had I added the fact that today's 25 degrees is almost five degrees warmer than normal for this time in November, although doing so might signal a certain ambivalence or feeling of dread.

You should know that at this time last year it was raining and colder than normal.

I needed to look this up, as I naturally assumed it had been warmer than normal at this time last year too.

It's good to be reminded that weather isn't the same as climate change, that change is measured over decades, and dependent on many unknown factors.

Scientists project that by 2100 the climate will be anywhere from 2 to 5 degrees hotter than pre-industrial times.

More than conflicting computer models, climate change is a problem of imagination.

James Watt never imagined in 1775 the changes his steam engine would drive.

I can't imagine what 420 parts per million of carbon dioxide looks like or how that traps more heat in the atmosphere.

I wonder if you can imagine what a rainy, cooler than normal day feels like.

My favorite technology these days is called *direct air capture*, which basically sucks CO_2 out of the sky and fixes it in the ground.

It takes more than 100 years for carbon dioxide to break down in the atmosphere on its own, but once it has been turned into rock, it will stay there for eons.

The most advanced installation right now is in Iceland and can capture 4,000 tons of carbon dioxide in a year, about three seconds of the world's annual CO_2 emissions.

Forty years ago, the world's first wind farm opened in New Hampshire, and generated enough electricity to power 30 homes.

Forty years from now there might be a lot of engines pulling carbon out of the air.

But now, in this moment, I imagine you taking a breath, taking in a molecule of my carbon with this sentence.

Kvernufoss Haibun

The waterfall grows insistent like a shard between my fingers as we hike up the canyon. Until every instant carries epochs leaping thirty-two seconds-per-second into cleft and pool. Photos have made this a place not to be missed, pilgrimage marked by taking, a reflex of want as bowing is to prayer. Point and shoot this view, even if that can't save the wind-borne spray, the tang of moss-covered basalt, the bone numbing torrent that unspools over our feet. Pixels will never hold the thrum of water pounding down, or catch the scale of it and everything around, so vast and insignificant. We know this, but keep snapping in case something sticks. There's a holy of holies behind the falls where the others climb for more poses, but I've come close enough. Go ahead, I say, the way is too slippery for me, and find a flat boulder to sit, offer my silence, my awe:

drops frozen
in an endless rush
glacial melt

The Glacier Guide's Lament

You could scatter us with an icy shrug
but I've stopped worrying about sudden disaster—
kids vanishing through unmarked cracks,
ropes snapping without scuffle or shout
from the back of the group.
Do you dream of thousand-year snowfall
in the flimsy dusk? Does fever carry you
far beyond moraine ridges
where raven calls shred in the wind?
I hope it consoles you that they visit
even if the miles crossed by air and car
are part of what's brought you to this.
They mean well, try their best to ignore the sick
on your breath as they march awkwardly in crampons,
gawk at the view, take endless pictures
as if that could stop everything.
Eons unstitch under their feet
and the chug of slush and meltwater in a moulin's maw
chases us long after the first drinks are poured.
Go home, I want to tell them,
while there's something left to miss.

Beyond Autopsy

After swallowing 25 shopping bags instead of squid, 115 plastic cups rather than a school of fish; after choking down a lone shrimp in a snarl of nylon strings; after dozens of soda bottles, drinking straws, a pinwheel and a sparkly pair of Mickey Mouse flip-flops that must have looked like mating crabs; after rotting for weeks in an ocean of jacuzzi warmth; after officials called in to *do something* pulled a parade of trash from its guts but wouldn't declare a final cause of death; after a village butchered what washed into the shallows; after fifteen men hauled the carcass ashore with hemp ropes; after the video went viral and was forgotten; after vultures and dogs were done; the bones of a thirty foot sperm whale opened to the sky and gave up the sea.

Eumillipes Persephone—The Leggy Queen of the Underworld

In other news, scientists recently discovered a millipede in Western Australia with a record 1,306 legs, making it the first millipede known to actually have more than a thousand legs. Using bore-holes left behind by prospecting mining companies, the research team lowered traps deep underground and waited a few months to see what turned up. The pale, string-like creatures drawn to bait made from decomposed leaf litter were of immediate interest. "As soon as I realized how long they were," one scientist said, "I knew this had to be something completely different."

Conservationists talk of different kinds of species. A *keystone species* is known for its outsized effects on an ecosystem, most clearly noticed when all hell breaks loose after being wiped out, or nearly so, by humans. See what happened when Pacific sea otters were almost hunted to extinction for their fur – they weren't around to eat sea urchins, which in turn allowed those spiky vegetarians to consume entire kelp forests, and in the process, spoiled the waters for multitudes of other supported life.

A *flagship species* is a charismatic animal with an outsized effect on human imagination, which among other things, helps raise money and public support for environmental causes. See for example, swag decorated with giant pandas and tigers, or how a half-gram migrating wisp of fire like the monarch butterfly sets peoples' hearts aflutter.

Which makes this particular millipede what? A blind, sweater thread snacking on fungi 50 meters below the Earth's surface is not exactly the stuff of carbon-neutral campaigns, yet here it is, washing up on social media and featuring in newspapers around the world. Is it simply nature's wondrous freak show that gives this story legs? Personally, I'm amazed by the wide-eyed curiosity that prompted someone to look in the first place, as much as the utter strangeness of what was found.

There's a third group called *indicator species*, named because they reflect the state of a given environment. Think of dragonflies zipping around a riverbank as a sign of clean water, or frogs disappearing from rain forests as an omen of even worse things to come. Only time will tell what *Eumillipes persephone* is trying to tell us – either that there will always be creatures getting along fine without us, or that there's no place left on this planet to properly hide.

On the Latest Reports of Global Warming

Washed ashore, Jonah waits all night,
slumped on a crumbling bench
empty beer bottle in hand,
deep summer a slack flag
desolate with cicada drone.
For hours the ocean tugs at his seams
and he longs to fold back
into its fathomless shade.
He dreads most the looming shrug,
all those slippered eyes and deadened ears
shuffling past his boardwalk perch
while a barker's taffy singsong
splits the daze with seagull cry:
breakfast special, five ninety-nine.

To a Polynya on the Longest Day of the Year

*Polynya (n): an area of open water surrounded by sea ice.
Borrowed by mid-19th century explorers from the Old
Russian word meaning empty or hollow.*

What I want is an explorer's hunger to name
every sun-slanted floe of ice,
to point north under midnight gloaming
and keep going until the next discovery.
What I want is a next discovery
not this thumb-scroll through the news.
Last week it was hotter in Siberia
than at the Dead Sea. This week wolf spiders
bore a second clutch of offspring in the Arctic summer.
Are the days not dire enough?
With so many facts I've forgotten how to feel.

Let me know you with sudden wonder
at unmapped expanse,
let me dive into you headfirst
and watch a bowhead whale surface for air, wait
until a snowy owl pounces on an eider duck.
Given enough time I would stay
and listen to the wheels of migration
swing beneath aurora curtains,
given enough time I could become like you,
far from any headline with the wind at my back
and a fathomless upwelling
beneath my feet, and in that parting
find a patch of open water.

Disappearing ABCs

And what might my children's children say
about their old board books and blocks
crammed full of catastrophic loss?
I never missed the dodo or eastern hare-wallaby
so why should they fret about unseen tree frogs
or mountain gorillas? Perhaps going is only gone
if you've heard honey-bees praise an almond grove
or sailed the sloop of an Indian elephant's back.
What if they flip past the Javan rhino and the killer whale
because they'd rather shiver when I roar like a lion?
I'll tell them lovestruck manatees sighed at the moon,
that dentists once knew how to treat
a narwhal's toothache, and if they don't notice
my sorrow over the orangutan, or believe
passenger pigeons flew in rivers across the sky,
then at least we'll question together what the quokka
ate for dinner. There really was a big bad red wolf,
until there wasn't. And some sea turtles
long outlived the dinosaurs, until they didn't.
Maybe the tiger with its simmering rage
will do what the umbrella bird or vaquita somehow can't:
speak to them from the dead, explain alongside
the whooping crane and wooly mammoth
what it means to be hunted until ex,
and why not even a zebra is left at the zoo.

The Death of Noah

Noah died in his sleep 350 years after the flood, at the ripe old age of 950. Some websites helpfully point out this was 2,006 years after creation, about 3,800 years ago by their count. They say archeologists found the outline of a boat on a mountain in eastern Turkey, proving Noah's existence. They say people lived longer back then because it was closer to the Garden of Eden and there were fewer things like viruses and cancer. My wife tells me helpfully that Noah didn't die because he never lived. You know that, right? You know the Torah is a moral guide not a history book. Noah didn't die but he didn't speak to me for weeks after getting wind of this, and I worried it would never be the same between us. Noah died when only one red rhinoceros showed up outside the ark. Noah gets teary-eyed when he tells me he never wanted to play the silent obedient type, but God didn't give him much choice. Noah died when the water pulled back like a crumpled sheet and the wind was bone bare and standing ankle deep in mud he looked up at the rainbow and God said don't cry everything will be alright. Noah didn't die but cried when he tilled the land and the grape vines he saved from before took root, cried every time he drank, cried every time he cursed his silent disobedient son. Noah says he didn't die, that he'll be there waiting when the animals come again.

Acknowledgments

Thank you to the editors of the following journals in which some of the poems in this book appeared, sometimes in earlier versions:

Coastal Shelf: "Beyond Autopsy"
Hole in the Head Review: "Sea Squill in the Garden," "Self-Portrait with Fainting Star," "Still Life with Unrolled Awning"
The Ilanot Review: "Disappearing ABCs"
Lily Poetry Review: "Evening Prayer"
Zocalo Public Square: "The Death of Noah"

Thank you to the Shaindy Rudoff Graduate Program in Creative Writing and Bar-Ilan University. Thank you to Marcela Sulak, Jane Medved, Joanna Chen, Sarah Sassoon, Mori Glaser, Bob Findysz, Joanne Veiss-Zaken, Elka-Hannah Yelenik.

Thank you to my parents, Barbara Hammer, may her memory be for a blessing, and Robert Hammer, may he live to 120; to Shirley and Howard Kossoy; to Michael Hammer; to Leora, Avi, and Shalom, who never cease to amaze; and to Meesh, for putting up with a poet in the ark.

About the Author

Poet, translator, and educator, Yoni Hammer-Kossoy's publications appear in numerous international journals and anthologies. Originally from Brooklyn, New York, Yoni has lived with his family in Israel for the last 25 years.

www.ingramcontent.com/pod-product-compliance
Lightning Source LLC
Chambersburg PA
CBHW070448130626
46553CB00006B/2309